It's Raining Toads and Frogs!

It's Raining Toads and Frogs!

Sue Wildgoose

First published in Great Britain in 2018 by

Bannister Publications Ltd
118 Saltergate
Chesterfield
Derbyshire S40 1NG

Typeset by Escritor Design, Bournemouth

Printed and bound in Great Britain

The Farmer's Wife...

Our small holding nestles on the edge of the Derbyshire Peak District. I've lived here for over 36 years and have worked the milk round with my husband, Mike, for the last 16 years. It is a life of long days, all with early mornings, but I consider myself the luckiest farmer's wife in the land, spending every day in such beautiful countryside, sharing our lives with our cows, pigs, ducks, hens, sheep, and more besides.

This little collection of words and sketches tries to show the ups and downs of farming life as we find it. The wonder of Nature ensures that the ups always beat the downs.

Of all the people I have to thank for their encouragement, our customers, many now friends, are our daily inspiration beyond the farm gate. Poetry is not an easy literary medium, and I am grateful to my publisher, Tom Blyth, for his belief in the work and his practical help at every stage of the process.

Finally, my thanks go to Mike and my daughters Helen and Anne for their patient support as I have wrestled the words and rhymes on to the page.

Contents

MILK ROUND ADVENTURES

A Thousand Sparkling Diamonds

A thousand sparkling
Diamonds, may light my path, but,
Carefully I must tread.

Busy

Busy, life hurries by.
Often laughter, sometimes, I cry.
Your presence, my world, does enhance.
Marvel at natures perpetual advance.

A February Morning

Small white van, picking its way up the narrow farm drive,
cutting through puddles of frost and ice,
headlights illuminating the dark, inky blue night.
Turning off at the village, my first customer in sight.

The engine softly growls to a halt.
I step out, catching my breath as the cold air bites into my cheeks,
disturbing an owl, who eerily tweets.
My torch, lighting the sparkling path I take;
my footsteps, treading softly up the first drive.
'Clink-Clink' as the milk on the doorstep, arrives.

Moving on through, methodically checking my milk book.
Reading notes: "Eggs please", "Extra Pint Today".
Up and down steps, winding my way, past
car roofs and windscreens, beautifully etched with white frost.
Black cat hesitates, then pads out of sight.
Guess he's been prowling most of the night.

Carefully closing the gate; don't bang the lock!
I hear the newspapers arriving at the shop.
Slowly climbing the hill out of the village, passing stone walls
and silhouettes of large bare, grey trees, hawthorn hedges, dormant,
waiting for Spring's call.

I see lights shimmering through the wood
from the houses beyond.
Cocooned in my van, with the radio on low,
last remnants of snow, reluctant to go.

Arriving at the estate, more deliveries to make.
On a nearby bough, a robin enthusiastically announces dawn.
I notice a handful of charming snowdrops, just peeping through a lawn.
When a solitary car rushes past me, late for work?

Distant church bells strike the familiar hour.
A blackbird crosses my path, then darts towards the doorway.
My fingers slipping, gripping the extra cold bottles today.
Dodge the paper boy on his bike, who smiles,
then peddles furiously away.

Now hear the traffic on the nearby main road.
A neighbour's softly spoken, "Morning", and I reply.
'Blaze' the fox terrier, tugs at his harness,
eager to greet, quivering tail.
"Hello Mate", as he sniffs, not keen on being fussed.
Curiously again, just to ascertain the contents of my van?

Last house – my round is complete.
Glance up at the new, silvery sky.
"Caw", "Caw", as a crow passes by.
Climb into my van, the road home,
I gladly take.
Confidently knowing my customers
have milk on their doorsteps
when they wake.

Milk Round

Forecast, heavy snow.
Freezing temperatures, zero and below.
On our service, you can depend.
Despite winter's elements to contend.
'Deliver milk to all', is our motto,
hopefully before 'cockcrow'.

Home

Icy fingers
Jack Frost lingers
Icy, bitten cheeks.
Wind, snowdrift leaps
Upon the gravel drive.
Cautious steps, I arrive.
Icy glass milk bottles rattle,
Tyres crunch, the road I battle.
Icy laden branch,
Flurry-does prance
Ice-etched stone wall.
Stoically, each customer, I call,
Icy breath-lungs inhale.
Wintry conditions prevail,
Icy toes complain,
Snowflakes find my bare neck again.
Progress, understandably slowed.
Ever dwindling load…
Icy farm track,
So … glad to be back.

It's Raining Toads & Frogs

Cool, dark, misty morning.
Spring is late this year.
The windscreen,
Constant rain, it smears.

Your feet – sombre light;
Careful where you place them.
Lest a toad, adventuring out.
A tasty worm or mate to chase.

Delve your hand into
that earthenware pot.
Surprised – suddenly – leaps a frog.
Hence the pint I nearly drop.

I peer into this muggy night.
That unsuspecting toad
duped me, thinking,
just a pebble in the road.

If you are up, very early,
see the milk-van weave:
"I'm not drunk".
Avoiding the little fellows
Is what I'm trying to achieve.

April Milk Round

Random street lights dimly glow.
My footsteps, accompanied
a whole orchestra of bird song.
Dawn reveals a delicious, pink-blue sky,
which tracks divide, as aeroplanes fly.
Daffodils wilt, now, past their best;
tulips, full height, vivid colours,
yet, unannounced.
Suddenly, loudly pronounced –
Honk! Honk! Reveals
a trio of flapping geese,
just above my head.
A black-white cat acknowledges my stare.
Her gaze, immediately transfixed – the handle:
imploring the owners within,
Please! Open the door!
Ornamental trees, delicate blossom
silently falls.
Oddly? Blackbirds form an avenue
either side of the grass verge.
Cold earthy scent – cut grass,
I ingest.
Sunlight highlights a roof, where a
wood pigeon rests.
He softly calls, "coo-coooo-coooo".

Magpie looks on, an egg cup
guards the cream inside
from that shifty eye…
All this transforming
what once felt like just an
Ordinary Morning.

No Milk Today

Legs, tired, aching.
Rain coat soaked.
Mind wanders to
Breakfast – belly spoke.
Comfy chair,
Warm fire, I stride.
Hot, milky coffee,
What fare? besides.
Wet fingers, milk book, smudge.
Next customer away.
Continue on into the estate.
Thinking about their holiday,
Somewhere warm, dry, not the UK!
Follow the road ahead,
Turn right.
All the way to the top,
Engine softly running,
As I alight.
Cold hands, two milk bottles,
Grip tight.
Almost forgot: six eggs, just in case.
Fiddle with the latch of garden gate,
Balancing all in a close embrace.
Keep to uneven brick-paver path.
Climb three stone steps to the front door.
Large white note I spy.

Carefully placing, 'pintas' on the floor.
Sticking out, high, from one of the many empties.
Intended not to be missed.
Soggy message pulled out.
Delicate order list?
Unfurled – bold letters,
Just starting to run.
What does it say?
Of course…
NO MILK TODAY!

Your Local Milkman

Traditional milkman, getting to be a rare sight.
Many deliveries made, well before light.
Their presence, detected by a small
Chink of glass, beam of torchlight.
"Milk in glass bottles"
"How quaint!"
"Didn't know they still existed."
But for a small band of loyal followers, milk book
enlisted.
"Maybe we should pay and save their DNA?
Endangered species, should be protected?"
There could be a time when plastic is out, and
The old ways, never quite dead, now resurrected!

Windy Day

Delivering milk today,
the wind, blustered, howled, played games
with me, stopping me in my tracks,
whilst pushing me onwards, then back.
Snatching the van door from my hand,
or closing it, with a loud bang.
Roaring past my ears,
then vigorously sweeps on, to seize,
shaking the nearby trees.
Its wrath, hiding empty bottles
halfway down the path.
Randomly blowing dustbins in the road,
Spilling newspapers, rushing out
on a tide of air, and surfing, rode
in spirals upwards, resembling a flock of birds.
To the dismay of a neighbour,
clad and clung in her dressing gown,
they target her garden, and land…
Desperately collecting all she can reach.
A single drinks can rattles across my feet, and I,
    gladly retreating, seek out the protection of my van.
    Let's leave this chaos, quick – that's now the plan.

An October Delivery

Sodium lights swathe my world; an orange glow
Softly cleaving the pitch black sky
As though etched with antique gold
Fallen leaves, lining where the pavement meets the road.
My warm breath, fog's, clashing with crisp, cold air
Sudden gust, leaves chase, then dance, before my eyes.
They settle, clinging moisture particles that my torchlight magnifies.
Small dark form hops around the doorstep, close to my feet:
A blackbird, yet not willing to fly.
Beech hedge, bordering a garden, shivers, trembles as wind sighs.
Disturb two black cats on the corner of the street.

Abruptly, their meeting ends, casting me such a scornful look as
They saunter slowly away.
Quietly, approaching the last block-paver drive –
Red brick house stands in darkness, silent…
Young family, all asleep.
Bending down, milk bottles I carefully place,
Not wishing to rattle any empties in haste.

"Are you there dear?" A stranger's voice, brittle with age.
In the poor light I freeze, my mind unable, the sound to locate.
The door handle moves, urgently up and down.
"Are you there dear?" The same trembling voice, but the door remains closed.
My heart thumps loudly against my ribs,
Catching my breath, unable momentarily to breathe;
Mind struggles to remain composed,
Knowing no one at that address to be old…
Quickly I retreat, and at the end of the path, I meet
What seems to be the same two cats;
Glowing, yellow-green eyes, and I'm sure,
A hint of a smile belies…
Feeling much safer in my van,
I remind myself as dawn breaks…
It's Halloween: strange things can happen, and no mistake.

Moment

The van steadily climbs the hill.
'Cotton Mill',
Just past the church yard gate.
I pause…
On the grassy headland above,
Silhouetted against the rising sun
Reddish-brown coat;
Solitary, proud.
Moisture-laden breath
Forms a small, delicate cloud.
Warm dark eyes stare.
A brief but memorable moment
We share.

SW

FARM LIFE

The Banty Cockerels

Heartfelt plea,
Could you take all three?
Banty cockerels,
I agree.
Charming addition
to our farm.
Vibrant coloured feathers,
Sun highlights in gold;
Small of stature but bold,
Puffed out chest.
Wings, vertical, vivid ruby comb.
Tail feathers, dramatic display,
as a gust of wind
makes play.
Drum, and plumage straightened
with a flick, like a fan.
Their plan,
Eyes sharp, ever alert,
Spying any tiny treasure
hidden in the ground.
Soft clucking soon brings
the girls around.
Presently, dominating the yard
with a shrill,
but familiar bard.

'Broody' Goose

At the end of the garden, by the fence,
The goose – laying a clutch of eggs, commenced
to settle, in her nest, that day,
covered, protected, with soft down and hay.
My daughter, not much bigger than knee height,
warned, "Not too close!"
Guarding her brood-birds, thoughts uppermost.
It would be… Yes, great idea! The clothes prop…
Useful length, became clear,
as prizing the goose up, to see beneath, I hear
flapping wings, chasing, hissing, out-stretched neck.
Ensuing howls, yowls, squeals… the effect.
Running swiftly to my daughter's aide;
angry bird retreating, now staid.
Only hurt, her pride, no one came to harm.
    But broody goose? Definitely, not one to alarm…
        Another one of life's lessons learnt.

I know a Goose

I know a goose, four husbands had she.
First, young love, strong and handsome he.
Dallied with a fox, a hero he made.
Defending his mate, his life he paid.

I know a goose, four husbands had she.
Second, all fierceness and hisses was he.
Ambushed, swinging on horses' fine tails.
To market he went without fail.

I know a goose four husbands had she;
Third, older, wiser, often would be seen,
Banned to the dog house, his lady, moody.
German shepherd, surprised, to share his kennel,
Just because she was 'broody'.

I know a goose four husbands had she;
Fourth. Patience and tolerance, the key.
Many happy years they have shared.
Loyalty, and a long partnership prepared.
'Soulmates', now completely paired.

"Dennis"

Dennis, quite a remarkable cat.
Adolescent challenges, put down with a pat
From a menacing paw, for being so bold.
Hugh, tawny tabby, of black'n'gold.
Treated as equals, human kind.
No better natured cat could you find.

Long hours, perfecting, hunting skills.
Notching up many kills.
Often seen, a wild rabbit, swinging between
His chest heading back,
Calling aloud, for the rest of the pack.

Used the ladder to gain the top of the barn.
Catching sunrays, while surveying *his* farm.
Or snoozing, curled on the tractor seat;
his habit of scent-marking this was a treat.
Not for the owner, who you wouldn't want to meet.
Wink, from an emerald-green eye,
as he sauntered along, tail held up high.

Considered it his job to inspect all vehicles;
Checking contents was quite typical.
Surprised the joiner one day, on a
trip to the DIY store, on his resumé.

Maybe this is what happened?
When he went missing, we were all saddened.
Had given up hope… 'til,
five months later,
our joy could not have been greater.
If only that 'Meow' could translate…

As deadwood, cut briars are collected.
Dennis' obsession for bonfires, erected.
Intense heat, whiskers affected.
Unperturbed, perched on a stone, he lay claim.
Silhouette visible, gazing into the dancing flames.
Staying to the last dying embers,
was always his aim.

The Guinea Fowl

Perched, proud, high on the shed roof.
Takes it upon himself to guard,
to sound the alarm
that echoes out around the farm:
Look Out! Look Out!
Reynard's about;
concealed amid
nettles, cow parsley, tall grasses…
Fair game, for him,
any innocent that passes.
Look out! Look out!
Seriously – don't doubt!
Summon the farmer, quick to defend,
and Cockerels! Quickly,
Rally our hens.

'Lucky'

Snub nose, upturned, squashed snout.
Pricked ears like bats.
Not the prettiest face.
Definitely an acquired taste.

Last one remaining
from a litter of ten.
'Lucky' was the obvious name
for her then.

Friendly, talkative,
with body quite stout.
Stands to be groomed,
with enjoyment, consumed.
Yard brush, stroking her back.
Emitting soft grunts,
as ears are scratched.

For sheer fun, she runs
alongside the dogs.
"Wuff!" She spins.
On again, she jogs.

Surprised, rabbit occupants one day,
collapsed, inwards, to their dismay.
Rubbing, against this hutch.
to satisfy an itch, was such.

Proud mum, but not one to enrage.
Amazing speed, she shows, for her age,
one squeal from a piglet, loudly made,
would bring her charging, straight to their aid.

Hungry, one morning, food late!
The orchard gate, rust and all rattles,
up on her snout, in one solid shift.
Helping herself to newly picked apples,
'All you can eat' of this welcome gift'

On those long sunny days,
often found in the shade.
'Mud Pack' in place.
Sleeping soundly, snoring loudly.
The good life, fully embraced.

Gather the Ducks

Gather the ducks,
'tis close to dark.
Always, the last to bed.
That said.
Never satisfied.
More of the field to explore.
Bills grubbing,
sifting, searching.
That extra morsel
could be costly.
Ever the opportunistic
Fox, moves softly.
Remember? Dangerous,
too far to roam,
        from the safety of home.
          At last! "All Occupants
          Accounted For."
       Now firmly close
that shed door.

The Lurcher

Intelligent, noble head, sleek of body,
Strong chest, set on long lithe legs.
Softly, how she treads.
Showing exceptional hunting prowess,
As she stealthily walks by my side.
Casting a watchful eye on any distant movement;
A word, a gesture, and the ground is covered with great speed.
Returning to me, with her gathered prize…
Relaxing by the fire, quiet, gentle, loyal.
Don't be fooled by those innocent eyes.
Surely they would tell you no lies?
When age catches up with her,
Sight is dimmed, legs a little stiff.
Asleep does she fall.
Remind her of hunting days,
with an old familiar call,
"Grace, *hi-loss*"

'Russell', JRT

Russell was a terrier, with a cheeky glint in his eye.
Confident tail, curled over his back.
Black, cute, button nose.
Founder of the pack.
Folded tan ears, set high on his head,
Numerous tricks, performed, if a biscuit was fed.
Remembering hours spent chasing an old stuffed sock.
Pretending, a rat, and running amok.

Memories of him, wedged between the children
In the big chair.
Captivated by cartoons on the TV.
All share the packet of crisps, perched on their knee.
One day, we called out his name, all over the farm.
Silence! Afraid he had come to some harm.
As it got close to dusk,
Found him, lying flat, surrounded by feathers, in the fox trap.
Guessed he was in trouble.
Tail held low.
Caught in the act,
That was a fact.
At thoughts of a reprimand, he would quickly disarm,
With a furious, wag of his tail
And abundance of charm.
Numerous ladies, from all over the local map,
Came to see this handsome chap.
So, today, if you happen upon a terrier,
With a familiar glint in their eyes,
There may be a hint of Russell;
You shouldn't be surprised!

The Old Ewe

Matriarch of the group.
Descendants follow the familiar track she leads.
Well acquainted with these
well travelled fields.

Crisp. Damp air, late autumn dictates.
Seeking shelter, as ambient light weakens.
Forecast many frosty nights ahead.

Carefully chosen spot.
Woollen back, propped against the hedge.
Partially protected by a canopy of sparse golden
leaves.
She gladly rests her old limbs.

The flock settles close by.
Content, her head lowers, eyes slowly close.
Thoughts drift to warmer spring days.
Taste of sweet grass,
Lambs full of vigour.

Cold, creeps, stealthily.......
Unseen.......unheard.......
Through these old bones....

At dawn's pink glow.
Sheep rise, stretch, one by one,
They gather, then slowly drift away.
The old ewe guides.

Strangely her joints, no longer ache
Each step feels light, free.
Unknowingly, her cold , motionless body
Still lies beneath the tree.

For 'Sweptback', 'Shorthorn', not forgetting 'Precious'.

The Fetch

Rapid ascent, the field she flies.
Sheep she holds with silent eye.
Inherent conversation in a wolf's guise.

Ewes yield, her path they shift.
Measured steps, controlled 'lift'
Insubordination given short shrift.

Working, driving flock down this sloping meadow.
Listening- weaving- nudging; constant flow.
Sheep pressed onward by this forceful shadow.

Nearing the holding pen.
It's gate the farmer clasps open.
This effective team, persuades this flock in.

All safely corralled once again.
Command ' That'll do'
Loving pat.
Her thank you.

T.B. Test

Annual T.B. test is upon us,
those with stock to sell.
We hear of cases nearby.
It's a worry, I can't deny.

Our Hereford cattle, corralled in the barn.
Gates tied in place.
The cattle crush in position.
Our local vet by its side.
Provided, I hope, with a safe place to hide.

First cow, eventually, persuaded to go in.
Grandad, gallantly holding the crush gate.
Mike deftly pulls down the yoke.
Not too late!

Which snatches her head, holding in place,
Whilst a small patch of hair, on her neck, is shaved.
The tuberculin skin test,
Administered at an accurate pace.
As one by one, ear tags are traced

Some, tossing their heads,
Object, protest with loud bellows.
"Watch Out!" One flick of a tail
Can hurl a generous
Mineral pack to your face.

'Mick' the bull, hangs back,
A little courage, he momentarily lacks,
An extra push and hearty shove,
Still one leg back.
Mike heaves once more,
Bull is installed,
Commenting, "He's a lot bulkier than I last recall."

Just one heifer to go.
Mike's dad announces, "We're making good time."
Our vet, as is his habit,
recounts old stories of past mishaps.
When the gate, behind, does collapse!

The cows, their weight multiplies,
To get to their offspring.
A shout, "Look Out!"
As a bullock squeezes by.

Crisis averted.
Thankfully, no body hurt.
Momentary lapse in concentration,
Can land you in the dirt.

Just three days to wait.
Procedure to run through again,
To check for reactors.
Removal and slaughter would be their fate.

I'm glad to report,
That all passed and are safe.
Many farmers are not so lucky.
Too many have the loss of a fine beast to face.

Rest

It's time to roost.
The highest perch gained,
you preen, fuss, dashingly spruced.
Get the top spot,
'You're made.'
Abundance of beautiful eggs, new laid;
announced proudly, with a loud cackle.
Disputes settled,
no need for rankle.
Every cranny and crevice of the
farmyard explored;
not a wisp of straw ignored.

Ever the keen eye,
no tit-bit unrevealed,
and quickly gobbled, with such zeal.
Dust bath, a ritual completed.
Feathers, combed, neatly placed,
Last sunray chased..
Now hasten! See darkness fall.
Seek the safety of the hen-cote all.
Huddled,
Settled,
Now rest.
For it won't be long,
'till the old cockerel's call.

Unpredictable Weather

Unpredictable spring weather
bringing sunshine, snow showers,
heavy rain, all together.
This year's lambing affected.
Our Wensleydale sheep, elected
to seek shelter in our barn:
straw bed, dry, warm,
the young safe from harm.
Shaking, bedraggled,
heavy curly coats, attack a rack-full
of sweet hay, their only desire.
Appetite of a small pony
they seem to acquire.
Next morning, bright,
Sun shining,
Ewes deep bellows,
Young, bleats combining.
Does make for a noisy parade.
Slow progress made,
With offspring at foot.
Tempted by springs
Fresh blades…

Suddenly! One ewe spins around,
Nearly knocking me down.
Back to the barn, she raced,
Searching for something, in haste.
I laugh! You forget!
You have not
Had your lambs yet!

Sorry Mate

Scouring the charity shop,
bumped into a burly guy.
"Sorry mate," his reply.
It's happened before
at the supermarket store.
The checkout, the man in front,
announced his vouchers could be
passed to "him".
Looking away,
I saw with dismay,
I was the only one in this queue.
Hesitantly, the assistant
handed them my way.
Now, noticing his mistake,
blustering, apologetic, red-faced.
Note to self:
Ditching the wellies, woolly hat,
before rushing out.
Maybe something
I should work at?

The Caretaker

Tread the same path,
Of so many before.
Stand on the same
Red and black tiled floor.
Touch the cool stone walls,
Hand-built,
Three centuries before.
Sleep in the same room,
Many others have rested.
Contemplate their lives,
Time invested.
Gaze through the window.
See the green fields beyond.
Smell the sweet hay-making.
Hear echoes, of bleats, bellows.
Clatter of milk churns.
Metal on horse drawn wheels.
Modern diesel tractor, engines.
Round baler,
'Winding', binding, plastic wrap,
Muck spreader,
'Whirling', hurling, fertilizing the ground.

Feel rain,
Soaking through your coat.
Imagine, wind
Rippling their faces,
The same welcome sunshine,
Warming our bones.
Recognise,
That sense of pride.
Lifetime,
Hold, over your heart.
Look closely,
See evidence of their toil.
And grasp that fierce attachment,
To these few acres of soil.
You are only 'The Caretaker'.
Leave all in good order.
Inevitably, when your time here ends,
You just might, secretly,
Visit this life again.

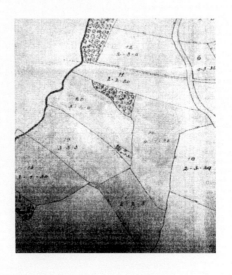

NATURE'S ENCOUNTERS

The Fox

Winter's sleep broken by a high-pitched scream,
Cuts like a sharp knife through my dream.
Time for the fox to court-mate,
as farm dogs bark, alarmed by the noise they make.

Dog fox emerges from cover close to the den.
Keen amber eyes, accustomed to the dimming light.
Recent shower of rain refreshing this spring night.
What a handsome sight!

He pauses, one foot hovering above the ground,
checking the breeze, ears twitching…
aware, intent, attuned to any small sound.
Shrill squeak of a vole grabs his attention,
there – hiding in a small tuft of grass.
Welcome meal, won with a high, crafty pounce.
One more not to pass.

Continues on, his calculated plan
to find food for his mate and new-born cubs;
helpless, all dependent on his return,
in their hidden, abandoned badger set, deep
among woods.

Artfully, he slips through the gap in the hawthorn hedge,
to skirt around the field.
Might it too yield
a rabbit? Strayed too far from burrow, tempted
by the spring grass, sweet and green.

Stealth in body, ears laid low, keen eyes detect.
Stalks towards the quarry, unseen.
A bird, startled, flutters in the branches above.
The young doe sits up, her instincts sensing danger…
and bolts, seeking safety in her burrow.
The fox denied his catch, the hunt foiled by a wild dove.

Trotting on, stopping here, there,
marking his territory.
Finds a beetle, an earth worm; though small,
all are welcome fare.

Then, risking all, heads for the farm.
The lure of poultry, so hard to resist.
From within the shed the geese hiss,
experience telling – the fox is about!
All awake now, and the dogs' wild barking
calls the farmer from his bed,
who, from his bedroom window, shouts.
Slickly, quickly, the fox abandons the task.
Luck's out, no hens tonight for Reynard's grasp.

Onward then, weaving his way down the stream.
Light roar of the water, swollen from recent rain.
Carving its way through the valley, untamed.
Pooling here, slowly trickles through mossy stones.
Fox, unbeknown, leaves small prints in the wet clay.

Steadily, on up the tall, grassy bank, he roams;
towards the gorse,
There's sure to be rabbits a plenty.
When he catches a scent – blood – feathers.
Caught on a breath of wind,
quickly alerting his senses.

Impulse draws him to this curious gift.
Wary of any human presence.
Falls upon a wood pigeon, shot earlier that day.
Tumbled to earth, with a soft thud,
Plume of feathers, white and grey.
Double-check for who's around.
Narrow muzzle, picks up the game,
and he's soon away.

Back to the den, quick as he can.
A short "wow",
greeting to the vixen, a rule to abide.
Much needed prize for all those lives inside…
Off, again,
much more to claim.
This, till dawn, his aim.

As spring turns to summer,
Family grown, be warned.
Both parents will be forced to hunt.
Let me be blunt.
You hear a magpie chattering, a caution,
warning, of his approach.
Cockerels' alarm call, gathering his hens.
Make sure your poultry are safely in their pens.

Many calculated risks will be taken
for the advantage of easy prey.
You might catch a glimpse of red, the tip of a white tail.
The hen's startled cry, growing ever fainter
as she's carried away.
That's the price we pay
to live alongside each other,
day by day.

The Hare

Crouching low in her form, long ears laid flat.
Perfectly still, camouflaged against the tussock of grass,
Intently listening.
Rich brown eyes, bright and knowing;
Nose twitching, capturing the wild scents brought in
On a gentle gust of air.
Early morning sunlight breaks
Through the last remnants of cloud,
To reveal a clear, blue summer sky.
The skylark, high above, sings a long familiar verse.
And a magpie's warning chatter cuts through the haze.
The hare sits up, stretching her athletic, graceful lines,
Sleek-coated beauty, ears erect,
Their black tips centering on any unusual sounds.
Her long, lithe body unfurls with a kick,
And a thrust of her powerful back legs,
She leaps forward, swerves, then vanishes…
This swift, illusive creature of many a myth and legend.
Protect her from harm,
For indeed, you may find she has a certain power to charm.

Gift

Hand crafted
From a fallen bough.
A mighty Ash,
Her gift, I endow.
Derbyshire field,
She proudly stands.
For centuries,
A fixture in the land.

Shepherd's Hut

Turn onto what was the 'old road',
Passing a row of tall poplar trees,
Swaying slowly,
Nudged by a light breeze.
Reaching the end of the lay-by,
Rumble over the cattle grid.
Glimpse the farm,
Green foliage amid.
Follow the drive,
Winding down through the field.
Silver birch in their wrought iron shields.
Disturbing a ewe
At rest on the warm gravel drive.
Calling her lambs;
On her milk, they thrive.
Pause a while, smile.
Resting there,
Its presence not amiss,
The shepherd's hut, a welcome sight,
Warm, inviting… what bliss!

Buzzard

Shrill haunting cry, as
Eyes strain, searching cloudless sky.
Observe… buzzards' gyre.

The Visitor

Listen! Hear him call.
Promptly he appears, there!
On the garden wall.
Marvel at this rich spectacle,
Generously embellished
With copious amounts of gold.
Surely, he's the one
Reared last year?
Hatched from an abandoned egg.
Grew into a quite unremarkable 'poult'.
Then mark such an incredible change.
Confident, he now parades
On my dew-covered lawn.
Lingers there a moment, then
A flash of colour – Gone!
Favour me another visit, soon.
Bring your princely robes,
And we can have our time, again.

The 'Taming'

Feel her breath…
Nostrils, slightly flared.
See the white of an eye
Wary,
Perhaps a little scared…
Neck muscles tense,
Approach with care.
Voice low…
Push forward,
Show the end of the lead rope.
Manoeuvre... slow!
Mirror her body
As she circles away,
Tossing head and bucking body high.
Ignore that, but with care,
Keep close, that shoulder angle,
Don't release, keep firm your stare…
Patience! The pace will ease.
Watch for the flick
Of an ear, listening,
The drop of her head.
Be calm.
Turn your body, slightly away.
Your rope must not tangle.
Will her first step towards you,
And eventually curiosity triumphs.

What a thrill!
If you are lucky,
She may nuzzle, and dark eyes soften.
Mutual trust… respect a must,
From this, the beginning.
No mistakes.
'Exmoor pony',
Truly natural, wild.
Give her time to adjust,
And rewards aplenty
Await us.

Dedicated to Kitty

Tree of Life

Today, I planted a tree.
A long, fruitful life I've
Planned for thee.
May your roots strike deep
Into the loam
Nature provided.
You, survive,
Indeed thrive…
Spring, beckons, budding leaves again.
Standing, steadfast, constant.
Years advance…
Many lives, you enhance.
Shelter, shade, provide,
Huge wealth of history, knowledge, you
must hide.
Our short existence, marked
With a ring, encased, within
Your heart.

From a Mother to a Daughter

'On her Wedding Day'

Dare I compare you to a precious gemstone, so rare?
Sensitive, thoughtful, but strong and so fair.
First born, irreplaceable, treasured, kind.
Memories of your childhood, forever in my mind.
Grown into a beautiful woman, adorned in splendour today.
A flawless, polished diamond in such a perfect setting.
Words are hard to say…
The jewellery box may be missing its most treasured gem.
Now in a bright surround, but never too far away.
My heart swells with pride and happiness for you this day.

For Mum

As daylight lengthens, in the early days of spring.
Snowdrops and daffodils, peeping through a new carpet of green.
Lambs, balancing on brand new legs…
You Are There.
Sweet, mown grass, drying in the warm summer sun.
Barns shielding newly mown hay.
Birds fervidly feeding their young.
You Are There.

Wheat and barley, stooping, heavy with grain.
Tractors, busy, late into the evening haze.
Autumn's wonderful palette of colours slowly fade.
You Are There.
Eerie, the call of the fox cuts through the cold frosty winter air.
Dogs, curled up in their baskets, dreaming of ancient hunting days.
Children's laughter, countless celebrations.
You Are There.
The lorry, winding down the farm lane before dawn awakes.
The milk van, climbing this hill as new light breaks.
You Are Here… in my heart
You Are Here… in the generations of family, your mark.

Remember Me

Remember me as the minutes gather into the hour.
At the end of the day, whilst gently drifting into a restful sleep,
Wishing you many happy dreams for you, to keep.

Remember me as spring unfolds its yellow symphony of daffodils,
Randomly decorating the bare floor.
Nature picking new life from its store.

Remember me as summer brings on a new dawn chorus of bird song.
Sleepy dogs basking in the sun, whilst bees are busy,
Seeking nectar all day long.

Remember me as autumn's trees cast off their robes
Of russet and gold,
Then curl and dance, as winds grow bold.

Remember me when the first white flakes fall, silently covering
The ground in a clean velvet cloak.
Muffling, painting a new world in one full stroke.

Remember me when you stumble upon a familiar fragrance or gift,
Instantaneously, your mind,
A captured moment does drift.

When a full and long life comes to an end, brimming
With memories, created in what seemed only a heartbeat.
If you wish, remember me, and I will be there for you to greet.

"Right Good Do"

What e'r wi du, thi' waint'g clammed.
Bin busy bak'in reet thru' neet
Dozens, cakes, pies 'n pasties,
Dunna wittle, av' a seat, Ther's
Enough snap, includin' bicuits an' all
Washed down wi' gallons o' tea
It'll be a reet gud do, yo'll see.